24/7

Keavd
Snoe

To order additional copies, please contact us.
BookSurge, LLC
www.booksurge.com
1-866-308-6235
orders@booksurge.com

24/7

Keavn Snoe

2006

24/7

This book is dedicated to my family and friends who have always been proud of me when I have succeeded and have never been ashamed of me when I have failed. JAT, CLL, BSB, SCS, LAH, TJJ, JVJ, LLW, MSL, RSS, RMS, MDS, KSV, MWJ, DAM, NG & JK.

A very special note of gratitude to my older brother: JDS. I miss you very much.

24/7

As I close my 24/7 and rest for the new one to begin
I take an inventory of the past one

I ask myself if I allowed my creativity to co-exist with my
    logic
Did I nurture it so that, like my logic, it can become part
    of me, unwavering and steadfast during those times
    when I need it the most

I ask myself if I strengthened my independence
Did I do things on my own that are a bit foreign to me
    and out of my circle of expertise or did I, once
    again, allow others to take charge of my life only to
    deal with the consequences of any mistakes that are
    made at a later date

I ask myself if I was supportive
Did I supply strength to friends during their time of
    weakness or did I apathetically sit by and watch them
    flounder in the quagmire of indecision and turmoil
    offering up only a rope of indifference as assistance

I ask myself if I was loving
Did I speak to others in a giving and understanding
    manner or did I offer my own woes and insecurities
    to others as gifts only to be self-righteous and
    indignant if they weren't appreciated

As I close my 24/7 I know only this

That a new 24/7 will begin tomorrow and I will continue
    to try

For those times that I succeed, I will be proud
For those times that I fail, I will learn

Keavn Snoe

AND YOU ARE?

Who are you to see through me
To discuss to define translucency

To monitor my thoughts, my every move
To grudgingly accept, to disdainfully disapprove

Who are you that you should care
The color of my skin, the length of my hair

The ones that I love, the ones that I hate
My rich deserving destiny, my sad and tragic fate

Who are you to make rules that bind
An open heart, an imaginative mind

A heartfelt touch, a caring soul
A giving laugh, a mournful toll

Who are you to decide what should be
Who are you, for I know

You are not me

Keavn Snoe

BARKING TREES

WILLOW SPOKE TO MAPLE
ON A BRIGHT AND SUNNY DAY
OF HOW HE WISHED HE WERE MAPLE
IN SO MANY DIFFERENT WAYS

HE WISHED HE COULD BE STRONG
AND FIRM AS MAPLE WAS
REACHING HIGH INTO THE SKY
FEELING THE AIR UP ABOVE

HE WISHED HIS LEAVES WOULD STRETCH
TO THE BEAMING RAYS OF SUN
HE WISHED HIS TRUNK WAS ERECT
IT LOOKED LIKE SO MUCH FUN

HE WISHED HIS BRANCHES LEAPT OUT
TOWARDS DIRECTIONS FAR AND WIDE
AND HE WISHED HIS FOLIAGE WAS FULL
WHERE CHILDREN COULD PLAY AND HIDE

MAPLE THOUGHT LONG
ABOUT THE WOES THAT WILLOW WEPT
AND FORMULATED HIS RESPONSE
WHILE WILLOW QUIETLY SLEPT

MAPLE ANSWERED WILLOW
ON A DREARY AND STORMY NIGHT
ON HOW BEING WILLOW
WOULD BE SUCH A WONDERFUL DELIGHT

HE WISHED THAT HE COULD SLOUCH
AND GROW A LITTLE MORE RELAXED
STRETCHING TO THE SKY
WAS FATIGUING TO HIS BACK

HE WISHED HIS LEAVES WERE LONG
AND TUSSLED LIKE SOME HAIR
HE WISHED HIS TRUNK COULD BEND
WHEN BATTERED BY ROUGH AIRS

HE WISHED HIS BRANCHES CAREFREE
WHERE HE COULD BOW AND BRUSH THE
    GROUND
HE WISHED HIS GREENERY WILD
HE WISHED IT WOULD DANCE AROUND

WILLOW LISTENED ATTENTIVELY
AND NOW HE UNDERSTOOD
THAT HE AND MAPLE WERE DIFFERENT
BUT BOTH WERE MADE OF WOOD

WILLOW REACHED OVER
AND BRUSHED MAPLE WITH GLEE
AND MAPLE STRETCHED UP HIGH
MAKING WILLOW GLANCE JOYFULLY

Keavn Snoe

BUOY

I cautiously wade out into the water
Sensing the warmth of the swirling currents
Around my ankles and then my calves
Splashing upwards toward my groin
Gently and tenderly

I settle into this new sensation
One of a distorted gravity
Where, like my body, my problems
Seem lighter, virtually unimportant
Considering the task at hand of
Staying afloat

I begin to timidly edge my way forward
Feeling the security of the bottom beneath me
Slowly creep away leaving but
Granules of sand between my toes
The latter stretching further downwards to
Maintain the connection with reality
With control

I am forced to begin supporting myself
With focused movements that soon seem
Less strenuous than I had originally perceived

The once solid and comfortable shore
Is becoming unrecognizable in the blurry distance
The familiar trees and assortment of beach equipment
Become faint splashes of color and shapes as

I continue my journey

In the endless distance ahead I can see another shape
I can hear sounds that, when listened to, are recognizable
As voices

Voices of encouragement
Voices that know my name
Voices that pull me onward effortlessly

As the object becomes clearer and more defined
I note that I am not alone
There are many here
Many whom I have never seen
But whom I know intimately
My arms are now moving on their own
My feet and legs generating energy
Without thought, without guidance

The distance behind me grows exponentially
While the expanse before my eyes becomes
A fluid balance of energy

I near the now visible object
It seems to be struggling
Dramatically out of sync with its surroundings
Frantic yet resolute

I take hold and a sense of calm ensues

I hear "thank you"

Keavn Snoe

BREEZE

I seek a breeze
to whisk away
the dust of indecision
that gathers in my head

The thoughts of wrong turns
or missed opportunities
pile up like
a thin film on the window
of my personality,
my being

A turbulent storm may suffice
temporarily
to fill this need
but I know that the aftermath
will only dry into streaks
hardening the once delicate and fragile
coating into harsh
symbolic tears that might
paint my face in
the darkened and lonely hours
of the night

I may remove the dust myself
with consistent diligence
a ritual cleansing
should time and will allow
but alas,

this becomes tedious

Just a breeze....

A breeze that I've felt
before on a spring day
after a long harsh winter

Where the sun is gently filtered
through clouds that one might
imagine serve as heaven's sofa

Where the temperature of the day
is equally inviting to shorts and a T-shirt
as it is to jeans and a sweater
one's own choice

Where the current of the wind
is soothing to the dryness of one's face
brought on by months of mother nature's
vain and jealous fury

Where one can imagine,
for a moment,
that he alone is a dandelion
near its beautiful end
to disperse from its familial
roots and take flight
landing
carefree and restful
wherever its chosen yet undetermined
destiny wills

A breeze

I seek a breeze

If for nothing else

To come and tussle my hair

Keavn Snoe

CITIZEN

He lingered on the corner
Hand outstretched
Quiet
Speaking only occasionally
And only with his eyes
Demanding nothing
Requesting dignity
Receiving embarrassment
His past life
Once regal and adventuresome
His present existence
Simply pauperized and hollow

Keavn Snoe

COMMUTING

The bright sunlight wakens me
A good half hour earlier than my usual process
I grumble at first but stop and reconsider

This day can be MY day

I spring forth and inhale my coffee
Sadistically enjoying the
Intense warmth that fills my throat

I hop into the shower and smile
Into the head as the beating water
Drives away all fatigue and
Exhaustion and energizes
My flesh

What to wear

My first choice has me gliding
Through the house
Oblivious to this Monday morning
Sensing more
A Saturday evening attitude

I stroll to my car and take
A different route than normal
Choosing to avoid the slow
Moving obstacles ahead of me

No parking available upon my arrival
I smile, shrug, and choose the next lot over
Knowing that I have Tori
To thank for the day

Knowing that my happy phantoms, too,
Can but nip at my heels for the balance
Of my waking hours

Koavn Snoe

ELEMENTAL

If I chose to be the fields
Would you choose to be the dew
Would you gently fall from
The early morning sky to wrap me in your arms
To rest casually on my upturned blossoms
Or to glide playfully down each blade of grass
To nourish me yet again and
Help me shine brilliantly in the dawn of a new day

If I chose to be the forests
Would you choose to be the fire
Would you run wildly about with your
Burning passion causing my greenery to disappear
In a blaze of vibrant colors
Would you slowly eat away at my protective
Shell to uncover the wonders within knowing that
What some see as destruction others call renewal

If I chose to be the oceans
Would you choose to be the moon
Would you linger gently above
Nearly motionless but all powerful
Effortlessly influencing my path, my highs and lows
Would you allow me to smile and reflect your beauty
To those around me who could simply stand in awe
At the union of the two

If I chose to be the air
Would you choose to be the breeze

Would you come along on a stagnantly hot afternoon
And pick me up to take me to a far off place
Would you carry me along your journeys
Laughing, smiling and dancing about without
Concern of what others might think of lack of rhythm
Or purpose in destination

If I chose to be me
I hope that you would choose to be you
And that we could enjoy one another
Without worries

Keavn Snoe

EQUILIBRIUM

Dulled sunlight creeps
into the room skillfully
as it seeks its slumbering victim

Pulling itself up the left side of the bed
it remains content in knowing
that it shall soon find its target
much like a missile finds its own:
unexpectedly startling its prey, hurling it
into a momentary period of panic
and fright until the moment passes

The difference, however, is apparent.
The sunlight's startled opponent awakens
to begin another day that will slowly
dredge on into a dreary afternoon
ultimately giving way to the uncomfortable closure of
nightfall

He will trudge through the day
growing sporadically more and more
curious about how the day's tasks
are going to be accomplished without
the presence of balance in his life

Equilibrium was a scientific theory
How could it ever have a hand
in his emotional state

Time had seemingly come to a halt:
An abrupt cessation of any movement:
Forward, backward, even laterally
like a severely myopic boy surrounded
by dim lighting without his corrective
spectacles he stumbles to and fro daily
asking himself the same questions repeatedly
without a final answer
a final destination

Tonight he will sit alone
comforted only by the same surroundings
that betray his desired mood
He will treat himself this evening
lounging, drinking, slowly purging
his mind of memories that can no
longer sustain him
Memories that serve as mechanical
tools of torture
that only cause pain

As he lies down for another
sleepless trance he glances one last
time as the moonlight shines dolefully
off of the withered and brittle deciduous
leaves that will soon fall and decay:
Another betrayal

He thinks solemnly of the cold
November rain
shivers slightly
and turns under the covers

to embrace his grim solitude
for yet another evening

Keavn Snoe

FAIR WEATHER AHEAD

This is to you
My fair weathered friend
Wherever you may lie
Wherever you may stand

I thank you for your time
And always for your words
Your sentiments, your feelings
Have clearly all been heard

The laughter in your voice
As your smile lights up your face
The sorrow in your eyes
As your tears streak your face

This is to you
My fair weathered friend
Wherever you may be
I am confident that you are the trend

Keavn Snoe

FAMILY TREE

Come to me
Let me embrace you
Let me share in the love that you share
Feel free to sit under my watchful eye
I will not judge
Bring your wife, husband, lover or mistress
It matters not to me what their color, gender or looks may
    be
Triviality is for the bushes to understand.
Let me explain
I am a tree.

Come to me
Let me suffer you
Bring to me your anger and I will not strike back nor
    shout
I will stand by quietly as you unload your pain and anger
    that has caused
You to hurt as you do
I will not wither from a few simple blows or wounds
Fragility is for the grass to consider.
Let me explain
I am a tree.

Come to me
Let me endure you
Let me comfort you in the times of woes and indecisions
Let my roots serve as firm examples that if you hang on to
    your

Beliefs long enough, then you will triumph
In the meantime, allow me to shelter you
From the tumultuous influences that may cause you
To waver in this troublesome time
Inconsistency is for the weeds to enjoy
Let me explain
I am a tree.

Come to me
Please come back to me
Let me err
My roots are always firm
My trunk is eternally solid
My branches offer you and your loved ones an
Unconditional love that no one else has
Why do you leave me
Where are you going
So I have lost my leaves
They will return
Let me explain
I am but a tree.

Keavn Snoe

FLUSHED

In your presence
The heat rushes to my face
As quickly as the day wakens over the oceans
Crisply welcoming another new experience

I hear the pounding of my heartbeat
As it begins to defeat the other senses
That I rely on daily
For balance

Visions dance wistfully in front of my eyes
As the room begins to toss back and forth
As if mother earth herself
Were boldly laughing at me

In your presence
I long to be the one by your side
Next to you, all alone in such a crowd not to be admired
But simply quiet and unassuming

Your touch breeds electrical sensations
That race the length of my body
Like a fast moving ripple on a small, motionless pond

Your voice comforts me, soothes me
Reminds me that fear is but a word
For which I can choose to be undefined

In your presence

I fall prey to my weaknesses
To my desire to be loved

In your presence

I am flushed

Keavn Snoe

I PREFER GRAY

Today I send my best wishes to all

To all who are so quick to accuse others
of failed and transparent attempts at control and
    manipulation
Likewise, to any who refuse even a feeble attempt to
    understand the impact of their words, advice and
    suggestions on others

To all who are true aficionados of therapy and self help
I admire not only their ability to label and name their own
    dysfunctions but their deep insight into even a total
    stranger's problems followed up with a diagnosis and
    a plan of action
Double kudos to their casual and flippant counterparts
    who are determined advocates of therapy atheism
They make denial less a moment or even a way of life
Like an artist with paint they color the day with a
    closed mind while appropriately labeling others'
    perceptions as simple excuses

To all straights who never attempt to see curves
To all gays who seem to deny the necessity of
    reproduction

To all who seemingly continue to repeat the same
    mistakes time and time again chasing others away
    while pulling closer and tighter to the question
    "why" to which there is only an answer of "because"

An equal bravado to those who disallow the existence of a
     trip, a stumble, even a minor infraction
To those who punish imperfect choices with harsh
     brutality, verbal or physical, or with just a simple
     basic rejection
How Original

Blessed are those that love as easily as most take a breath
Where love is not earned or compounded like interest but
     over abundant, overflowing and all consuming
To those, as well, who avoid the aforementioned
     personalities of the world:
loathing their naiveté
scoffing at their frivolity
mostly, however,
fearing themselves

To those who never turn down an invitation to drink
To those who never accept one

To those who endeavor, devotedly, to be honest and pure
     in their motives
Who question not only every one of their own actions but
     everyone else's as well
Likewise to those who are completely oblivious to the
     concept of the subconsciousness and prefer to live
     with "IT" being the primary subject of each sentence
     that they speak

Congratulations to those that have the "I" passive
     perfected
And to those who believe fervently in the "You"
     aggressive

In my experiences in life I have seen a variety of colors

The rainbow that adorns the sky is but a simple example
of diversity in a world so complicated with black and
white

In my life I have seen many shades

And

I prefer gray

Keavn Snoe

IF ONLY

If only I had a little girl to call my own

Her smile would sparkle like a brilliant star
that shines on the coldest of northern nights
while at the same time
bringing the most comforting warmth to fend off the
    unrelenting chill

Her eyes would burn like a soothing heat
that warms the back of my neck as I walk along a
    southern beach
looking out over the ocean and thinking about my place
    in the world

Her energy would run like the endless sun
that travels all night long to greet me on an eastern
        morning never too tired from its journey throughout
        the evening to bring me the joys of a new day

Her hair would whisper like a quiet dusk in the western
        sky
that ushers in the end of another day, never too abruptly
but instead comfortably easing me into nightfall with a
        gentle reminder that dawn will return

Her personality would intrigue me like the Manhattan
        skyline
with wonderment on its past, present and unwritten
        future

Her curiosity would remind me of how I have pondered
        my own purpose in life
understanding that the mark that I leave on this world is
        based on the choices that I
make in life and to choose very carefully

If only I had a little girl to call my own

If only she could be just like you

If only

Keavn Snoe

LIT

When my reality blurs into the likeness of a faded cloud
I look towards you, towards your light

When my vision fails to guide me from the sad doubt
That stalks me regularly with each move that I make
I believe that yours will help me to see my way clear of
The faint and subtle shadows that I have mistakenly
Asked to dance

When my spirit forgets the presence of its wings that
Assist me in my daily travels through the heart
I believe in your ability to teach me, once again, how to
Seize the breeze and take flight

When my conscience refuses to ignite my confidence and
Instead burns the fallacy of others' comments into my
        mind
I believe that yours will soon be present to protect me
        from
These diversions like a warm quilt offering not only
        security
But serenity as well

Whenever my reality may blur into the likeness of a faded
        cloud
I will always look towards you

I have been lit

Keavn Snoe

MEMORY LANE

In a moment of unreasonable
Panic
He stumbles through the crowd
Frantically
Searching for the one that his
Mind
Can't remember but which his
Heart could never forget
Visage after visage passes
Before his eyes
At a pace that recognition
Cannot match
He desires to stop those
That resemble even the
Slightest characteristics
From the crooked smile to
The cocked brow
But realizes how
Hopeless this would be
As well as damaging
He realizes his illogical panic
For what it is
And fears that it shows in his
Features
But even more he worries that
It will begin manifesting
Itself at an
Exponential rate
Causing those around him

To gawk and jeer
He settles for glances
Knowing that those that
Glide by as small boats
Skim the surface of a
Calm pond
Are only reminders of
What he no longer has
What he has lost to a loving vice

Keavn Snoe

MIDNIGHT SNACK

When my day begins with a chilled floor from
    unexpectedly cool weather the night before
When my commute to work takes me past winding roads
    and confused drivers
When my arrival at work is met by problematic voice
    mails
I drink a cup of clouds and take a spoonful of orange
    marmalade

When the reality of a bad decision is highlighted by a
    monetary loss
When lunch refuses to be quiet
When one more meeting cannot fit into my head
I drink a cup of clouds and take a spoonful of orange
    marmalade

When all I can think about is the comfort of my home
When I dread opening the mailbox to see yet another
    demand on my resources
When I know that laundry must be done
I drink a cup of clouds and take a spoonful of orange
    marmalade

When I know that a relationship has reached an impasse
When I know that my body is lacking its youthful
    strength
When I feel that I just want to cry
I drink a cup of clouds and take a spoonful of orange
    marmalade

Whenever I am faced with a challenge
Whenever I know that my actions do not reproduce as do
    my consequences
Whenever I am saddened by a change that I know is a
    must instead of a want
Whenever I realize a mistake cannot be corrected

Whenever

I drink a cup of clouds and take a spoonful of orange
    marmalade

How refreshing

Keavn Snoe

MY ANNIVERSARY

Today on my first anniversary
I am reminded, like all others,
of a very special day

What stands out to me, however,
are some unique differences

My day will not be celebrated with
fresh flowers that adorn the dinner table

Ironically it will be spent taking care of
a potted plant that was given to me
just one dry day away from death

I took that plant and repotted it
I've nurtured it and spoken to it daily
to ensure that it grows solid and its
greenery full to provide me shelter
in preparation for the time,
should it ever come,
that I require it

My day will not be celebrated by
committed words shared with a
chosen partner in life

Instead I am reminded of the
rude and abrupt introduction to a
stranger who would, here and forever, be

my houseguest

A relationship has been forged:
one of mutual respect, I think

We manage through our daily lives
without interrupting one another

We have, in a strange way, devoted ourselves
to ensuring that we do not have to pick up
after one another

My day was not a reward of
years of careful planning and investment

My day was a consequence of a momentary
indiscretion and a highlighter to
so many mistakes where punishment
seemed cumulative

I've wrestled him to the ground and held
him solid until both of us were tired

I've listened to his words
carefully and without accusation

I have noted where it was that I went wrong
and have set myself onto a solid path of learning

In return he has assured me that the cumulative
effect will be lessened through our mutual agreement

This is my anniversary

No more, no less
than any other

Simply a different foundation

To me,

To us,

I say

Happy Anniversary

Keavn Snoe

MY LIFE

Try as it may my novelty does not wear thin
It does not grow old and brittle
With the years as do my bones
It does not obtain blemishes as does my skin
My novelty stays fresh and untarnished and much like
     stainless steel
Creeps in and plays the inexperienced for the fool that
He or she will soon realize that they are

I am the trinket on the mantel that everyone
Wants to see, know its inner mechanisms but is leery
Almost fearful to touch
I am the one in a crowd who no one understands yet who
     everyone knows I am
The awkward
The soulless
The disposable part of society once I have outlived any
     usefulness that others may have or hold for me
     assuming that there is that utility.

But do not despair or sympathize for me
I know my station
Up on the mantel set aside not to bother those that are
     mainstream
I am to be different and acknowledge that which sets me
     apart not to forget or wonder
Or even worry

What other role would the gods or lords of destiny have
       me play
This is me
I am gay

Keavn Snoe

MY MIND'S EYE

My mind's eye
Has opened wide
To see what lies ahead

My life unfurls like a March sky
In the early morning
With the clouds rolling backwards
To clear the way for the blueness
     (different from winter when clouds seem to sink into
     the blue)

I see the joy of joining with a partner for life
I see the pleasure that this person will bring into my life
I feel the heat as it rushes to my ears from his mere
     presence
I feel the tears as they roll down my cheek from the first
     betrayal
I feel how my heart swells with love during the
     reconciliation
I experience the comfort that I receive from growing old
     and frail with my
partner
I sense the fear grip my heart as I grow concerned for his
     health and
welfare
I endure the inaudible beats in my own heart
As he is lowered away from me down, down
And I see myself recover and move on towards my own
     end

My purpose

My mind's eye
Opens wide
And I see what lies ahead

Now I only wait
For my life to unfurl
Patiently

Keavn Snoe

MY SCHIZOPRHENIC HERO

My hero lies in the eyes of he who understands the value
    of a total stranger's life
yet is recklessly dangerous with his own

My hero is embodied in a woman in her late thirties who
    embraces the challenge of getting her college degree
    and is able to see it as fun and exciting
as opposed to a cumbersome burden

My hero lies in the lips of he who will speak the truth
understanding all too well the typical results and
    consequences of doing so

My hero does not deny his depression
but selectively chooses to ignore it when it is inconvenient

My hero lies in the body of he who has taken time to
    sculpt and mold his physique into the finest of
    quality
yet erroneously has forgotten to nourish his mind as often

My hero lies in he who can acknowledge the she
and in she who does not squabble about equal time

My hero lies in the determined and structured actions of
    a young man who strives to keep pace with a frantic
    world successfully maturing and growing
while only widening the gap between himself and his own
    generation

My hero lies in the voice of he who stands up for the
    underdogs of the world
and shouts out declarations regarding the inequalities
that he sees through his myopic eyes

My hero lies in the courage of the young man who cruises
    his own mortality at such a young age
and foolishly tampers with the workings of greater forces
    than he

My hero lies in he who silently watches a loved one make
    a mistake
and, when asked to respond, will simply say "did you
    learn anything"

My hero lies in he who believes in his jealousy
only enough to give it a label

My hero lies in he who, beyond all chances, strives to do
    what is right in his own heart knowing all the time
    that those contents could change tomorrow

My hero's voices are varied, his body quite diverse

His heart
Part of me

Keavn Snoe

PALE BLUE

Your presence is likened to that of a cloud

On a soft summer's day

I see you as you hover in the air gently caressing the pale
blue of

The afternoon sky

Not roughly but soothingly as if you were larger than the
sky itself and not

The contrary

You endlessly take on shapes of

Visions that are always imagined but never materialize

Shapes of sweet blossoms that yet exist

Of edifices without structural definition

Of liquids that dance of their own volition

You remain out of reach, distant, always teasing with a
calming smile

I do not fear or anger

For, as night falls, I know you will descend to soften the
    harshness

Of the evening's

Obscurity and darkness

Keavn Snoe

PAPILLON

Just a single gust of wind
As a child
Seemed to pick up my dreams and hopes
To scatter them about wistfully
To be wild and out of reach
I enjoyed watching them flutter about
Highlighted by the brilliant sun

As a young adult I fought hard
To capture them, to hunt them down

I found myself placing them
Like a collector of butterflies
Behind a pane of glass
To keep them tidy and free
From any outside influences
They served as a point of admiration

As I grew the dreams remained
Unchanged
Offering less solace and comfort
Over time

Opening the glass cage that had
Held them for so long was
Without question a more challenging task
I had to use caution
I had to ensure that they were strong
Enough to withstand the forces of a changed

Environment
I wanted to continue to protect them
Seemingly denying that they were not only
Durable but had actually grown in strength
Knowing that one day I would set them free
To flutter and flit around again

As I now chase them it is not to capture them
Or to protect them
It is I who simply follows
With a smile on my face

It is I who is simply along for the ride

Keavn Snoe

THE PARK

I strolled to the park today
looking and waiting for you to meet me

You did not show

I patiently bided my time knowing and
believing that your smile would greet me
from a distance that only you and I would understand

You did not show

I believed that as you slowly and casually approached me
that our eyes would lock and speak to one another from
a past that seemed to hold only us
all alone
to breathe in one another's exhales

You did not show

As others walked by I gazed dolefully at them
and whenever their eyes met mine I would turn
away
Not in shame or embarrassment but just noting
that it was not you

The day seemed to lumber slowly along
as the heat burned down upon my shoulders
reminding me of the moments (no, the lifetimes) that
had passed since our last visit

You did not show

Alas, I realized that and
I began my journey home again down the
busy street trying to shake the disappointment
from my heart like a dog shakes the excess water
from his body

I felt reassured, having done this
that one day

You will show

Keavn Snoe

VISIBILITY ZERO

The rain would not cease
The sun sang karaoke through
The pale white and gray clouds
Often stopping when the lyrics were forgotten
Pausing for multiple musical bridges

The trees danced effortlessly to an understood melody
Acoustical thunder synchronized the brightly
Fashioned lightning produced by mother earth herself

The terracotta color of the bricks came to life
As the rain rescued them from a heated drought
That was soon to claim more victims

The surface of puddles rippled along with
Glee unconcerned with the intrusion
Of the bucket-size drops of rain that
Tried, in vain, to shatter their smooth surfaces

The rain cascaded down at all angles leaving nothing
Dry for fear, not brutality, of being chastised later
Of leaving someone out

Leaves upturned to greet their salvation were
Quickly stricken down into a position of
Complacency, even capitulation, without complaint

The clear surface of the pool changed from bright white
To dark turquoise in scattered places dependent upon

The driving force of the sheets of water during every
    fraction
Of a second, slowly the music died down to a slow
Melodic beat and couples took to one another to express
Their joy and love for having experienced such a great
    moment
In both solitude and companionship yet, when all is done
    and the sun returns our thoughts to reality

I rain

I cry

Tears

Not for having feared the moment

Not for a grateful sigh and relief that it has passed

Nor even for a longing that it shall return expeditiously

I cry tears

For those whose only conscious description
Of the moment could ever be

Visibility Zero

Keavn Snoe

VISIONS OF FALL

As I lose myself in those soft brown eyes
I am reminded of autumn

I am reminded of how the beautiful and lively
Green leaves seem to surrender to the
Seasons once again
And fade from a forest green to an amber red
And then to a singed yellow

The tarnished hue hangs on
Holding steadfast to a place it wants or
Needs to call home
But understands
That it cannot

The brown arrives
Not suddenly so as to frighten its surroundings
But slowly and gracefully
As a ballerina glides onto stage
During a tragic scene

She is not there to save anyone
Nor to interfere in the impending doom
She is only present for the audience
She serves to assist the guests
In making sense of such a
Pointless loss and tragedy

Her presence allows the sharing

And interpretation of what has just
Been witnessed

So functions the soft brown in your eyes
They serve to mirror life in a distorted
Manner

One in which pain is always accidental
And not to be understood
By individuals
But more as a
Collective whole

Keavn Snoe

VISITING HOURS

The darkened angel peers in my window
I hear the slow, methodic tapping but
Willfully ignore the hypnotic sound
As I continue on my regulated pace
I have several projects yet uncompleted
So my uninvited visitor remains ignored
And distant
I have not yet felt my lungs bulge
From proper, uncontrollable laughter that I have
Promised myself
I have not yet felt my hands tingle
From the touch that convinces me that how I
Feel is right
I have not yet felt my lips brush life
With the on-the-edge-of-my-seat sensation
That I have read about
I have not yet felt that warm presence next
To me on the coldest night of the year
I have not yet allowed myself to experience
These things
Only as a reminder
That my visitor is still
unwelcome

Keavn Snoe

WHEN DARKNESS HIDES

When we are at our weakest moments
and our faculties and senses seem completely unreliable

when the words that escape our palates are
betrayed by the tears that fall from our eyes

when the concept of heartache becomes
a fearfully tangible reality

when the day seems obscure and
the night comforting with its folded arms about our souls

when the truth to others seems implausible
since the truth to ourselves is certifiably impossible

when we fail to set our own standards
and live by those imagined that others may hold for us

this is when darkness hides

deep within

to frighten us away from the light

Keavn Snoe

WONDERMENT

It is with admiration
That I look into your eyes
And envision your strength

It is with affection
That I touch your hand
And grasp your warmth

It is with excitement
That I taste your lips
And savor your passion

It is with tranquility
That I smell your scent
And inhale your serenity

It is with adoration
That I hear your voice
And ascertain your patience

It is with wonderment
That I lie next to you
And absorb your presence

And

It is with disappointment
That I note there are but
Five senses with which

I can experience you

Keavn Snoe

WORDS

The words that are locked up inside my head are many

I want to shout to the world that understanding and
      compassion
should be placed before ignorance and spite

I want to whisper to the lovelorn that victimization is but
      a creation
of their many choices in life and that extraction is a
      strength
not a weakness

I want to preach to the pitiful and the sorrowful
that this is all but cyclical and that their time will come
in another consciousness

I want to belittle the small minded and controllers of the
      world
so that they too can understand that the food chain of the
      world
does include them and that they are not at the top of it all

But most importantly, sometimes
I just want the words to go away and only say

me

Keavn Snoe